621.3 Billings, Cha
B   Fiber optics

D0573609

DATE DUE		
FE 5 '89		
AP 29 '88		
MY 27 '8		
JA 0 6 89		
MP		

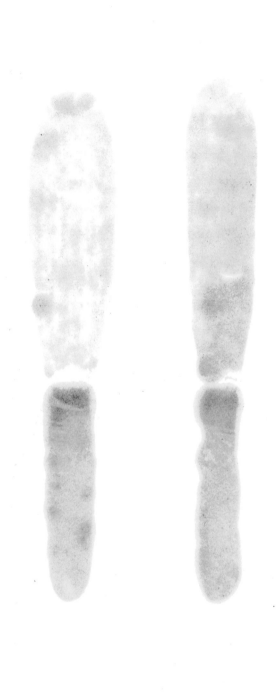

Fiber Optics

Bright New Way to Communicate

WESTWOOD SCHOOL LIBRARY
SANTA CLARA UNIFIED SCHOOL DISTRICT
SANTA CLARA, CALIFORNIA

ECIA-CH2-86-87

Fiber Optics

*Bright New Way to
Communicate*

Charlene W. Billings

A SKYLIGHT BOOK

Illustrated with photographs

DODD, MEAD & COMPANY
New York

For Sharon

PHOTOGRAPH CREDITS

Courtesy of AT&T Bell Laboratories, page 2, 6, 8, 9, 10, 15, 17, 19, 20, 45, 47; Courtesy of Corning Glass Works, 14, 39, 40; © The Walt Disney Company, 18; Courtesy of ITT Electro-Optical Products, 11, 23, 25, 31, 32, 37, 38, 41, 42; Furnished by Nippon Telegraph and Telephone Corporation, 22, 55; Courtesy of Reichert Fiber Optics, Southbridge, MA., 26, 27, 28, 29; and United Technologies Building Systems Company, 12, 58, 59.

ACKNOWLEDGMENTS

My sincere appreciation to everyone who has helped to provide information and photographs for this book. Special thanks to those who answered specific technical questions about fiber optics during the preparation of the manuscript.

Copyright © 1986 by Charlene W. Billings
All rights reserved
No part of this book may be reproduced in any form
without permission in writing from the publisher
Distributed in Canada by
McClelland and Stewart Limited, Toronto
Printed in Hong Kong by South China Printing Company

1 2 3 4 5 6 7 8 9 10

Library of Congress Cataloging-in-Publication Data

Billings, Charlene W.
Fiber optics.

(A Skylight book)
Includes index.
Summary: Discusses the history, manufacture, operation, and future of optical fibers, used as a method of transmitting information through light.
1. Fiber optics—Juvenile literature. [1. Fiber optics] I. Title.
TA1800.B55   1986   621.36'92   86-4548
ISBN 0-396-08785-X

FRONTISPIECE. *Pinpoints of light emerge from glass fiber used in lightwave communications systems.*

Contents

In Bell's photophone, sunlight was bounced from a reflector through a lens to a mechanism that vibrated in response to speech.

1
What Is Fiber Optics?

In 1880, four years after he invented the telephone, Alexander Graham Bell tested another talking device. He called it the photophone.

"Photo" and "phone" come from the Greek words for "light" and "sound." Bell's telephone used pulses of electricity traveling over copper wires to carry sound. But the photophone used a beam of sunlight traveling through air to carry the human voice from one place to another.

Bell was very enthusiastic about the photophone. He wrote to his father, "I have heard a ray of sun laugh and cough and sing!"

Bell's photophone was exhibited in the National Geographic Society's Explorers Hall in Washington, D.C.

However, the new invention did not prove to be very practical. Sunlight was only available during the daytime. And even then, bad weather such as fog, rain, or snow blocked the beam of light.

In spite of these problems, throughout his life, Alexander Graham Bell thought the photophone was his most promising idea. He felt certain that someday people would use beams of light to talk to each other.

For nearly one hundred years, scientists like Bell dreamed of using light to communicate. They knew that light and electricity traveled as vibrations or waves. And they knew that many more light waves could be transmitted in one second than electrical waves. For this reason, light could carry more information than electricity flowing in copper wires.

Not until the 1960s and 1970s did two inventions make the dream possible. During this time, scientists invented *lasers*. Lasers are powerful sources of a special kind of light. Other researchers developed *optical fibers*.

A laser shown in the eye of an ordinary needle.

Workers at Bell Laboratories, Rich Linke, left, Joe Campbell, center, and Byron Kasper, appear next to reels of lightguide fiber, transmitter, and receiver.

An optical fiber is a flexible thread of very clear glass—thinner than a cat's whisker and up to six miles long. Laser light can pass through the length of an optical fiber and still stay bright. Because optical fibers can serve as pipelines for light, they also are called *lightguides*.

In the mid-1970s, these inventions were teamed together. Now pulses of light flash through optical fibers carrying information and messages over great distances. This important new technology is called *fiber optics*.

Glass fibers are replacing copper wires for many reasons. The fibers are not as expensive for telephone companies to buy and install. They weigh a lot less than copper wires — making them easier for workers to handle. A single four-and-one-half-pound spool of optical fiber can carry the same number of messages as two hundred reels of copper wire that weigh over sixteen thousand pounds!

Spool of optical fiber cable.

Private branch exchange switch.

Optical fibers also take much less space than copper wires. This is very important in crowded cities where bulging, overloaded telephone cables have little room for additional lines. Optical fibers can help unsnarl this telephone traffic jam.

The fibers are better, too, because light is not affected by nearby electrical generators, motors, power lines, or lightning storms. These often are the cause of noisy static on telephones or information errors in computer systems connected by copper wires.

As electrical signals pass through copper wires, they become weakened. Devices called *repeaters* are used to strengthen the electrical signals about every mile along each line. In a fiber optic system, repeaters are needed only every six miles or so to boost the light signals. And experiments have shown that this distance can be stretched many more miles. This means that installation costs for a fiber optic system are less now and can be cut further in the future.

However, the most important reason for using glass fibers is that they can carry much more information than copper wires. A single pair of threadlike glass fibers can transmit thousands of telephone calls at once. A cable as thick as your arm and containing 256 pairs of copper wires would be needed to handle the same number of conversations.

A single glass optical fiber can carry the same number of telephone messages as the wire-copper cable containing 256 pairs of wire.

Pairs of fibers (or wires) are used for two-way communication. One fiber carries your voice to the listener at the other end of the line. The other member of the pair transmits the other person's reply to you.

Optical fibers are less expensive, easier to install, and more dependable than copper wires. With light from a laser, they can transmit thousands of times more information than electricity in copper wires. The new technology of fiber optics is a better and faster way to communicate.

This optical circuit can carry over ten thousand voice signals.

2

Where Are Optical Fibers Used?

All over the world, the copper wires of telephone trunk lines are being replaced by modern glass optical fibers.

One of the first attempts to use an optical fiber system in the United States was in 1977 in Chicago. There, two offices of the Bell Telephone Company and a third building for customers were connected successfully by twenty-four light-carrying glass fibers. The fibers were threaded through telephone cables already under the city streets. The total length of the fibers was about 1.5 miles.

In 1978, Vista-United Telecommunications at Walt Disney World near Orlando, Florida, was first to use

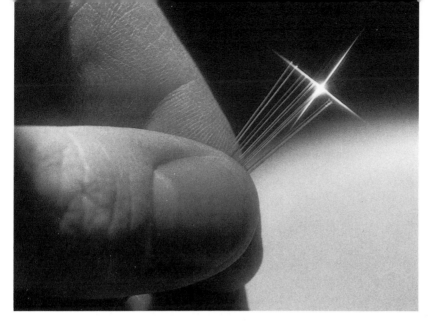

Twenty-four hair-thin lightguides used to carry Bell System customers' voice, video, and data traffic under the streets of Chicago in 1977.

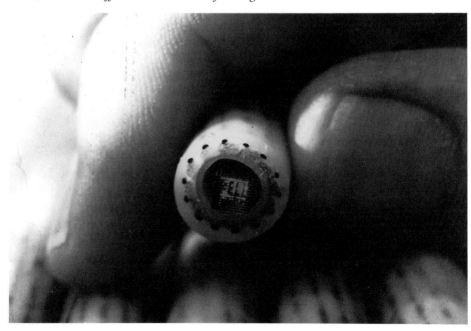

A fiberguide cable is used to carry voice, television, and data signals. This cable contains 144 glass fibers.

fiber optics commercially in the United States. Telephones throughout the 28,000-acre park are linked by fiber optic trunk lines. Video transmissions by glass fibers are made to many individual hotel rooms on the property from one location. Lighting and alarm systems also use optical fibers.

In EPCOT Center (Experimental Prototype Community of Tomorrow), there are information booths equipped with television-like, two-way video screens and speakers. The screens and speakers are connected by optical fibers to a central office. A visitor can activate the screen by touching it and select the information

Central computer system at EPCOT. © *The Walt Disney Company*

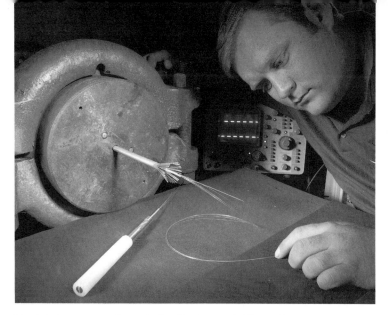

Al Quigley, a member of the Undersea Cable and Apparatus Design Department, examines optical fibers emerging from a pressure vessel simulating undersea conditions. Such work has helped to pave the way for the first Trans-Atlantic lightwave cable to go into service in late 1988.

needed. Or the guest can talk to an operator who appears on the screen if requested.

American Telephone and Telegraph has in service a fiber optic trunk line that connects Boston, New York City, Washington, D.C., and Richmond, Virginia. The trunk line is part of a project 780 miles long. The light cable used is only about the thickness of a garden hose. Nevertheless, it can carry eighty thousand calls at once.

By July, 1988, American Telephone and Telegraph will have laid a fiber optic cable beneath the ocean between North America and Europe. The cable is called

The world's first deep-sea test of lightwave communications.

TAT-8 because it is AT&T's eighth *t*rans*a*tlantic *t*ele-phone cable. TAT-1, a copper cable, was completed in 1956 and could carry fifty-one calls at a time. TAT-7, the last copper cable, was laid in 1983. It can handle about eight thousand calls at once. TAT-8 will transmit forty thousand calls at one time. Even with TAT-8, a second fiber optic transatlantic cable, TAT-9, probably will be needed by 1991. Another undersea cable, between California and Hawaii, is planned.

The Japanese telephone company, Nippon Telephone and Telegraph, has placed glass fiber cables from one end of the country to the other. By 1990, similar lines will join Japan to Hong Kong, Australia, and New Zealand.

A fiber optic system in Munich and other cities of West Germany is called Bigfon. It transmits a video picture along with voice. In addition, Bigfon sends and receives copies of documents and other important papers.

Over fifteen hundred customers in Biarritz, France, use videophones and television channels made possible by fiber optics.

In the remote countryside of Manitoba, Canada, two towns are part of an experiment. Elie and St. Eustache have become "glass-wired" communities. Optical fibers connect keyboards and television sets in homes in these towns to distant computers. People who live there use the keyboards to get television shows, radio broadcasts, weather forecasts, news, farm and stock market reports.

WESTWOOD SCHOOL LIBRARY
SANTA CLARA UNIFIED SCHOOL DISTRICT
SANTA CLARA, CALIFORNIA

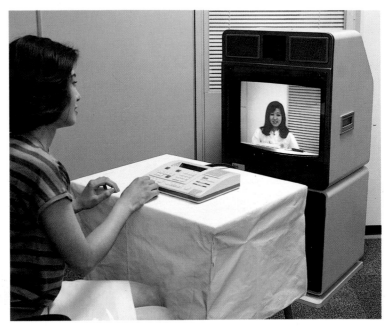

Video telephone in Japan.

In addition, over three hundred items for sale at a large, well-known department store, Hudson Bay Company, can be viewed on television. To make a purchase, a customer types an item code, number of items wanted, size, color, and credit card number on the keyboard. Hudson Bay Company receives the order and ships the goods directly to the customer.

Near Tokyo, in Japan, there is an optical fiber communications network known as HI-OVIS (Highly In-

Fiber optic telecommunications being installed in Saudi Arabia.

teractive Optical Visual Information System). With this two-way system people can take an active part in educational classes such as piano lessons. They also can learn about schedules for airlines, trains, and concerts, and get up-to-the-minute news and weather reports.

New installations for communications at Kennedy Space Center in Florida use fiber optics. These include the Space Shuttle control center and operations building for Launch Complex 39. In addition, the Space Center's fiber optic system is used to check out experiments, such as those on board *Skylab*, before launch. Eventually, all of the facilities for the Shuttle at Kennedy Space Center will use fiber optic systems.

There are many other uses for fiber optics. A medical instrument known as an *endoscope* is made from bundles of optical fibers packed inside a long, slim, bendable tube. A doctor slips this medical "spyglass" into a patient's throat, stomach, lungs, or intestines to look for anything abnormal. One bundle of fibers carries light to the tip of the probe. Another bundle of fibers transmits pictures back to an eyepiece. This allows a doctor to see inside the human body without surgery. And sometimes it locates early stages of serious diseases, such as cancers, that X-rays may miss. Miniature tools within a separate channel in the endoscope tube can remove samples of tissue for a closer look.

A physician uses a fiber optical medical lightguide.

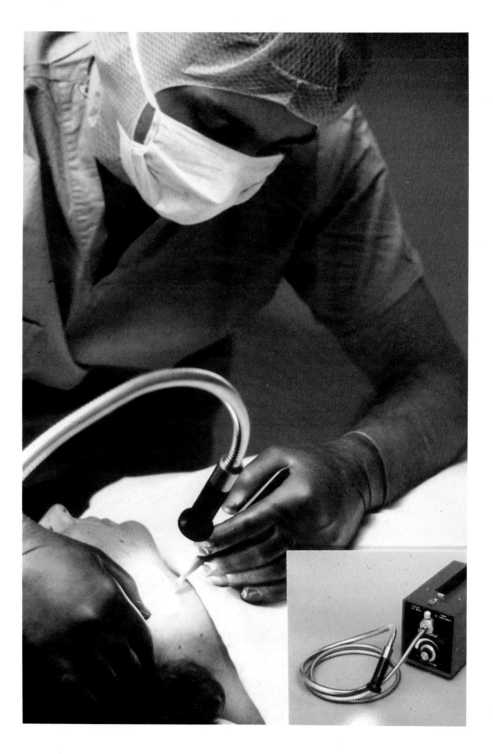

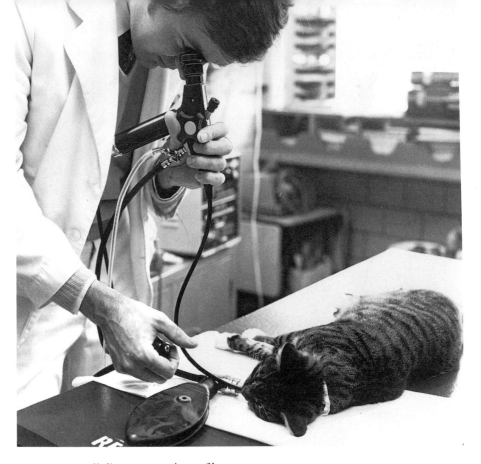

A small diameter veterinary fiberscope.

Veterinarians examine horses, cats, dogs, and other animals with similar fiber optic scopes. Pets sometimes choke on foreign objects. With the probe of the scope, the animal doctor can locate the object, snare it, and quickly remove it.

People peer into dangerous or hard-to-see places with industrial fiber optic scopes too. Workers can look inside

Aircraft engine inspection with an industrial fiberscope.

and check radioactive reactors in nuclear power plants, the jet engines of airplanes, turbines, boilers, pipelines, gear boxes, and many other types of machinery.

An image conduit and clad rod.

Image conduits are large pipelines for light. They are formed from thousands of optical fibers that have been bundled and fused together into one unit. They can directly transmit images or pictures from one place to

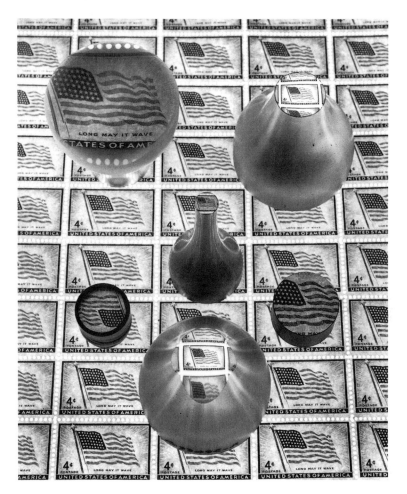

Fiber optic tapers, couplers, and inverters.

another. If the conduit is tapered on one end, it can be used to make an image larger or smaller. And if the fibers in the conduit are twisted, the picture can be turned upside down.

Wafer-thin plates sliced from fused bundles of optical fibers are used to make night-vision goggles or scopes. The plates are treated with chemicals that enable them to magnify moonlight, starlight, or any other available light thousands of times. With the goggles, U.S. Forest Service helicopter crews can spot even small embers on the ground that could start a fire.

Individual optical fibers guide light from one source to many switches and displays on the dashboard of a late model automobile or the instrument panel of a recently built jet fighter. The fibers are small and lightweight. And they are not bothered by other electrical equipment fitted closely behind the dash or panel. In some cars, optical fibers monitor parts of the car. They signal the driver if a light burns out or if a door is ajar.

Many kinds of sensors are made with optical fibers. These devices can detect changes in temperature, pressure, or the presence or absence of something. Different sensors can check for a wide range of things at factories—from missing caps on soda bottles to toxic fumes. They help guide robots or other automatic

Fiber optical cable being installed aerially.

Fiber optical cable being buried.

machinery to manufacture items as intricate as electronic circuits or as large as automobiles.

Glass fibers are ideal for military defense. In addition to their other advantages, the fibers are easy to hide from an enemy. Metal detectors cannot locate them, for example. Also, the fibers are almost impossible to secretly tap or jam. Thus, vital messages are more likely to get through. Light-carrying fibers usually are not affected by radiation. And they can be used safely near ammunition storage areas or fuel tanks because they do not create sparks as electricity can in copper wires.

The North American Air Defense Command is located deep inside Cheyenne Mountain in Colorado. Its computers, linked by optical fibers, process radar information from around the globe. Army field communications systems also depend on optical fibers.

Optical fibers are being used by the University of Pittsburgh to connect school computers. A college student or teacher will be able to get information from any connected computer, library, or classroom on campus. Other schools are installing similar networks.

The new technology of fiber optics has grown quickly in the past decade. In the next ten to fifteen years, the copper wire telephone trunk lines in most of the world will be replaced with glass "wires." These slender strands will harness pulses of light to transmit the human voice and vast amounts of information in a twinkling. More and more, people will use beams of light to communicate with each other.

Imagine how excited Alexander Graham Bell would be to know that his dream has come true.

3

How Are
Optical Fibers Made?

The glass used to make optical fibers must be very pure. Light must be able to pass through the length of the fiber without being scattered, or losing brightness.

Though the glass in an eyeglass lens looks perfect, a three-foot-thick piece of this kind of glass would stop a beam of ordinary light. Tiny particles of iron, chromium, copper, and cobalt absorb or scatter the light.

The glass in an optical fiber is nearly free of impurities and so flawless that light travels through it for many miles. If ocean water were as pure, we would be able to see the bottom of the Mariana Trench, over thirty-two thousand feet down, from the surface of the Pacific.

An optical fiber has a glass inner *core*. Light travels through this highly transparent part of the fiber.

The core of an optical fiber is surrounded by an outer covering called the *cladding*. The cladding is made of a different type of glass from the core of the fiber. For this reason, the cladding acts like a mirror. Light traveling through the core of the fiber is reflected back into the core by the cladding — much like a ball bouncing off the inside wall of a long pipe. In this way, light entering one end of an optical fiber is trapped inside the core until it comes to the other end.

How do people make these gossamer threads of glass that can carry light around curves and corners and over long distances?

Optical fibers are manufactured in "clean rooms." The air in these rooms is filtered to keep out the tiniest particles of dust. Even the smallest specks of dirt could ruin the fiber as it is made. Workers in these areas usually wear jump suits or lab coats and caps made from lint-free fabric.

Tube before layers are deposited, hair-thin fiber in center, and preform on right.

An optical fiber starts out as a hollow glass tube. The tube is mounted on a machine that rotates it. A special gas is fed into the tube. A flaming torch moves back and forth along the tube, heating it to nearly 1,600° C. With each pass of the torch, some of the hot gas inside forms a fine layer of glass on the inner wall of the tube. A

Technician in clean room garb monitors collapse of a preform.

series of different gases can be fed into the tube. With this method, layers of several different kinds of glass are added to the inside wall. When the addition of glass is complete, gas still inside the tube is gently sucked out.

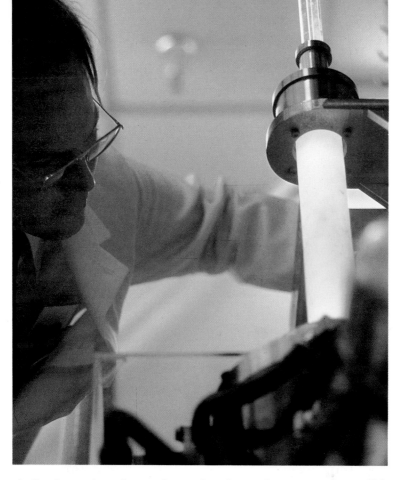

A Corning engineer lowers glass preform into a draw tower, from which hair-thin optical fibers are drawn. Heat from the draw tower lights up the preform.

Now, the heat from the torch is increased to 2000° C. The hollow tube collapses into a solid glass rod called a *preform*. The preform is the size of a broomstick — about as big around as a fifty-cent piece and a yard long.

*Optical fiber, used for voice, image, and data transmission, is being drawn
from the draw tower.*

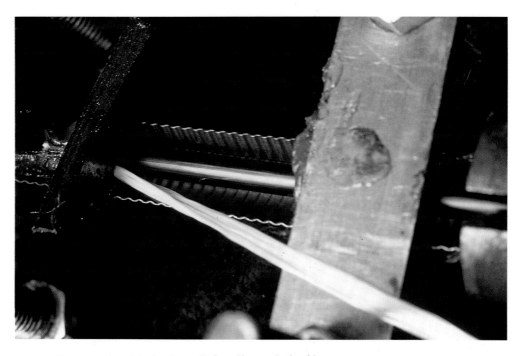

Corrugated steel jacket is applied to fiber optical cable.

The preform is cooled and carefully inspected. Light from a laser is used to make sure the core and cladding of the glass preform are perfect.

Next, the preform is placed in a special furnace where it is heated to 2,200° C. At this temperature, the tip of the preform can be drawn or pulled like taffy into a wisp of an optical fiber — thinner than a human hair.

Usually, as soon as it is drawn, the fiber passes through a tiny funnel where it is coated with fast-drying plastic.

Quality control engineer tests fibers.

The coating protects the fiber from being scratched or damaged.

The fiber from a draw may be up to six miles long. It is wound onto a spool for ease of handling and storage.

Glass is usually thought to be brittle, unbendable, and easily broken. Amazingly, optical fibers are flexible and strong as threads of steel. The fibers can be tied into loose knots without breaking and light still passes through from end to end.

4

How Do Optical Fibers Work?

Whenever you talk to someone else the sound of your voice travels to their ears as a pattern of vibrations or *waves* in the air. Light and electricity also move in waves.

To get an idea what waves look like, tie one end of a long rope to a post or tree. Hold the other end of the rope and walk away until the rope is stretched out, but still slightly slack. Now yank the free end of the rope up and down repeatedly. A series of bumps or waves travels down the rope.

You can change the pattern of the waves. You can make small waves by giving weak, up-and-down yanks on the rope. Or you can make big waves by giving strong, up-and-down yanks on the rope. The height or tallness of the waves depends on the strength you use to yank the rope up and down.

The distance between the top of one wave and the top of the next wave is called the *wavelength*.

Another way to vary the waves is to change their speed. You can yank the rope up and down only once in a second or many times in a second. The number of waves reaching the tree or post each second is the *frequency* of the waves.

Why do pulses or waves of light streaking through an optical fiber go farther, better, and faster than electricity pulsing through copper wires?

Lasers used in fiber optic systems are made from tiny crystals of a material called gallium arsenide. These lasers are as small as a single grain of salt and easily could fit through the eye of a needle. Nevertheless, they can produce some of the world's most powerful pinpoints of light.

Light from a laser is unlike ordinary light. Laser light is all of the same frequency and wavelength. And all of

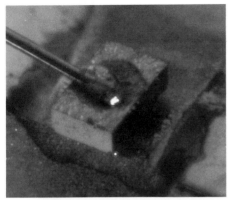

Close-up of a gallium arsenide laser.

Loops of a hair-thin glass fiber, illuminated by laser light, represent the transmission medium for lightwave systems.

it is traveling together in the same direction — like bullets aimed from the barrel of a gun at one target. The result is a brilliant source of very pure light. Laser light can shine through miles of optical fiber without being boosted as often as an electrical signal.

The laser light used in fiber optic telephone or communications systems is *infrared*. The frequency of infrared light is just below what people can see with their eyes unaided. Infrared light is used in communications systems because it can travel long distances through optical fibers with less loss of power.

Another source of light that also is used with optical fibers for communication is a *light emitting diode* or *LED*. LEDs are less costly than gallium arsenide lasers. However, lasers can transmit more information at higher speeds than LEDs.

Copper wires can carry a few million electrical pulses each second. But the number of light pulses an optical fiber can carry is much greater. It is limited by how many pulses of light each second today's best lasers can produce. Recent experiments done at AT&T Bell Lab-

Bell Laboratories developed this long-lived, long-wavelength LED, which is used in the Sacramento lightwave system.

oratories combined the output of several lasers to achieve as many as 20 billion pulses per second! This far outshines the number transmitted by copper wires.

How do telephones connected by optical fibers work?

In the mouthpiece of a telephone, the pattern of sound waves of your voice is first changed into a pattern of waves of electricity moving through copper wire. In a fiber optic system, a special electronic device called an *encoder* measures samples of the waves of electricity eight thousand times each second. Then, each measurement of the waves is changed into a series of eight ON-OFF pulses of light.

The pulses of light are a code that stands for the strength or height of the waves of electricity. This is called a *binary code* because it uses only two signals or digits; zero for when the light is OFF and one for when the light is ON. The word "binary" means two. Each zero or one is called a *binary digit* or *bit*. And each pulse of ON-OFF light stands for one piece or bit of information. Eight bits grouped together are a *byte*.

The specks of ON-OFF light flash like tiny comets through optical fiber carrying your message in binary code.

At the other end of the line is another device called a

decoder. The decoder changes the pulses of light back into electrical waves. The receiver of the telephone then changes the electrical waves back into the sound waves of your voice.

The coded pulses of light in a fiber optic system can carry so much information so rapidly that many telephone conversations can be stacked in an optical fiber. They are then unscrambled at the other end of the line.

Because a fiber optic system uses coded pulses of ON-OFF light, it is ideal to link together computers. Computers "speak" this binary language. They not only count in binary, computers also store and handle huge amounts of information as a code of zeros and ones. The entire 2,700 pages of *Webster's Unabridged Dictionary* can be transmitted from one computer to another over optical fibers in six seconds!

Morse Code is a binary code you may already know. Instead of zeros and ones, Samuel Morse used dots and dashes to send any message by telegraph. The dots and dashes can stand for any letter of the alphabet or any decimal number.

Here are two binary codes. One is International Morse Code and the other is a computer code known as the American Standard Code for Information Interchange or ASCII-8.

Character	Morse Code	ASCII-8
0	-----	01010000
1	. ----	01010001
2	. . ---	01010010
3	. . . --	01010011
4	. . . . -	01010100
5	. . . . .	01010101
6	-	01010110
7	-- . . .	01010111
8	--- . .	01011000
9	---- .	01011001
a	. -	11100001
b	- . . .	11100010
c	- . - .	11100011
d	- . .	11100100
e	.	11100101
f	. . - .	11100110
g	-- .	11100111
h	. . . .	11101000

Character	Morse Code	ASCII-8
i	. .	11101001
I		10101001
j	. ---	11101010
k	- . -	11101011
l	. - . .	11101100
m	--	11101101
n	- .	11101110
o	---	11101111
p	. -- .	11110000
q	-- . -	11110001
r	. - .	11110010
s	. . .	11110011
t	-	11110100
u	. . -	11110101
v	. . . -	11110110
w	. --	11110111
W		10110111
x	- . . -	11111000
y	- . --	11111001
z	-- . .	11111010
. (period)	. - . - . -	01001110
?	. . -- . .	01011111
!	--- .	01000001
, (comma)	-- . . --	01001100
" (quotation mark)	. - . . - .	01000010

Can you figure out what the following message says? First it is given in International Morse Code; then in ASCII-8. Alexander Graham Bell said these words in the first telephone message to his assistant, Watson, on March 10, 1876.

.-- .- - ... --- -. --..--

-.-. --- -- . ... . .-. . .-.-.-

.. .-- .- -. - -.-- --- .- ---.

10110111	11100001	11110100	11110011	11101111
11101110	01001100	11100011	11101111	11101101
11100101	11101000	11100101	11110010	11100101
01001110	10101001	11110111	11100001	11101110
11110100	11111001	11101111	11110101	01000001

ANSWER: Watson, come here. I want you!

Morse Code and ASCII-8 may seem awkward. But Morse Code made possible sending messages quickly by telegraph over long distances as early as 1845. Today, computers linked by optical fibers can send vast amounts of any kind of information, including pictures. And they can do it faster than the human mind can think.

5
Fiber Optics in the Future

Many scientists think that the technology of fiber optics will lead to an enrichment of life like that following the invention of the steam engine, light bulb, and computer.

Only a small number of homes, businesses, schools, hospitals, and libraries in the world are connected by optical fibers now. But as fiber optic technology develops there will be an enormous expansion of use. In the future, fiber optics will make affordable a wide range of services that may be too expensive for most people or businesses now.

An example of this is teleconferencing. Rather than

Teleconference in Japan.

travel far from their companies and homes, business
people will more commonly meet by teleconference.
They will send live television pictures of themselves to
each other and talk as though they were in the same
room. AT&T, Western Union, and some hotels already
have teleconferencing rooms for rent in many major
cities. However, in 1984, the cost was over $2,000 an
hour. But soon it may cost as little as $30 an hour.
Further in the future, fiber optics may be used with a
method called holography for teleconferences. Holog-

raphy uses lasers to project three-dimensional images of people or things into thin air—no viewing screen is needed. Laser images transmitted by glass fibers will be so lifelike they will be hard to tell from the real person or object.

Some researchers dream of building an optical computer. The "brains" of today's computers are microchips. These tiny electronic devices are only as thick as a thumbnail and one-quarter inch on a side. Within, they are a maze of miniature metal circuits and thousands of special switches known as *transistors*. Pulses of electricity passing through the microchip's circuits and switches process all of the computer's information.

An optical computer will operate using pulses of light passing through optical switches. The transistors in a microchip are fast—they can switch ON or OFF millions of times each second. But scientists have built experimental optical switches that are ten thousand times faster. They can switch ON or OFF an incredible one *trillion* times each second!

Supercomputers of the future operating at faster speeds would make possible automatic translation of foreign language telephone calls (such as English to Japanese). Optical computers also would be the best way to transmit or process highly detailed visual information such as photographs or maps.

In an optical computer, switches will be able to process many bits of information at the same time — something electronic computers usually do not do. Because of this and their faster speed, optical computers would be far more powerful than the computers we have now.

With fiber optics, individual homes and businesses will have new, improved services available. The future will bring routine use of videophones that allow callers to see and hear each other. Telephone consoles may also be computer terminals. And there will be two-way television reception.

Fiber optic sensors will send information to automatic controls for lights, heat, air conditioners, appliances, or industrial machinery. Police and fire fighters will give better security to homes and businesses that have sensors connected directly by optical fibers to monitors at headquarters.

Someday you may work in an "intelligent" office

City Place in Hartford, Connecticut.

building. The building itself may look much like other offices. But inside will be a world of difference.

The first of these office buildings is City Place in Hartford, Connecticut. Others that already have been built include Tower Forty-Nine in New York, LTV Center and Lincoln Plaza in Dallas, Texas, and Citicorp Center in San Francisco. By 1990, over 300 million square feet of "high I.Q." office space is expected to be in use.

An "intelligent" office building has fiber optic detectors that "see" if people are in a room before turning lights on or off. The detectors are connected to a main computer that regulates heat, ventilation, air conditioning, and lighting in each office of the building. Such automatic

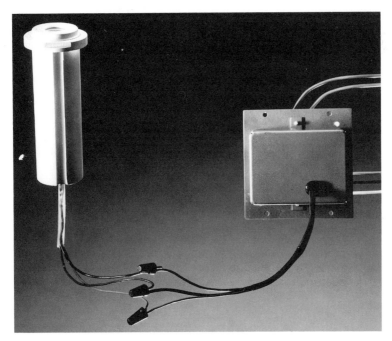

This system turns office lighting on and off as it detects and responds to changes in radiated heat caused by the presence and movement of a human body.

controls in large buildings can save as much as one-half on energy usage.

Just as important is that businesses in an "intelligent" office building share the benefits and costs of the most modern computer information networks, electronic mail, word processing, and telephone service. These services have been designed into the building's fiber optic system.

Security in "intelligent" office buildings also is improved. If, for example, a sensor detects a fire, its signals automatically ring alarms, call the fire department, activate sprinklers, exhaust smoke to the outside, and broadcast emergency instructions.

Fiber optics is lighting the way to an astonishing information age. Home computers will be "wired" to the world. Information from libraries and other sources will be available to us instantly. Banking and shopping will be done from home as well. Electronic newspapers, magazines, and mail will become commonplace. Telephones will be fitted with sockets to plug in computers, printers, television screens, and other information transmitting or receiving devices.

Away from Earth, new uses for fiber optics also will be found. In the 1990s, the National Aeronautics and Space Administration will build a permanent space station. It will be in orbit about three hundred miles up. The space station will use on-board fiber optic systems for communications, computer processing, monitoring, and controls. The station also will establish factories in the near-zero gravity of space. Some of these factories will manufacture glass more flawless and free of impurities than can be made on Earth. This ultrapure glass will be brought back to Earth by the Space Shuttle to be made into even better optical fibers and other products.

Sometime in the next century, people will live in space colonies. They will process information and communicate using optical fibers and light. And they probably will find uses for fiber optics that haven't yet been imagined.

Alexander Graham Bell's brightest idea will have become a reality reaching far beyond his most fantastic dreams.

Index